Also by Joan Morris Reilly

A Hungry Hill Trinity

Other Voices, Other Times....Hungry Hill Remembered

ST. CASIMIR'S CHILDREN

The Lithuanians of Westfield

JOAN MORRIS REILLY

dedicated to

Josephine Minkle Morris

For your courage and your
example,
Ačiū, Senelė

Acknowledgments

This book was inspired by family members who have passed on. My father and his sisters and brothers were people with a simple philosophy on life. They believed in working hard and playing hard. Every one of them loved to sing and were terrific dancers. My father and two of his brothers were accomplished self-taught musicians They played chromatic harmonicas. The three of them often played all night at social gatherings.

Because of these gatherings, my siblings and I knew the words to numerous songs from the 1940s. To this day, if I happen to hear "Til we meet again" or "Long Long Trail" or "Sentimental Journey" on the radio or tv, I get tears in my eyes. In addition, my Aunt Ann and cousin Lete showed us Lithuanian dances and shared many stories from the past.

Whenever I write about my ancestors, I regret very much that I never thought about writing when my aunts and uncles were still with us. Who knows what they could have added. This book is dedicated to my grandmother, Josephine Minkle Morris. Even though we never met, her inspiring story of personal courage is a reminder of the caliber of people who went before us.

I am grateful to Natalie Masaitis for sharing memories of her Lithuanian heritage (special thanks for the beautiful linen towel and hand knit socks from Lithuania) and a very happy 100th birthday to this amazing lady. I am equally grateful to Jim and Marcia Rogers for sharing their knowledge and stories about St. Casimir's Church and Knights of Lithuania Council 30. When I told them my maiden name, they instantly knew the Lithuanian version of Morris.

As always, I am thankful for the support of my children, Jim and Beth and their respective talents of editing and photography. Many thanks to my brother Dick Morris and his perfect recall. Also, the contributions of Joe Christofori, Chris Murphy Photography, Carol Akialis and my late cousin Michael(Champ)Morris, were very much appreciated. In addition,

Lituanus, the Lithuanian Quarterly Journal of Arts and Sciences provided some very relevant excerpts and information.

PREFACE

We who spent our early lives in the shadow of immigrants should know that every old neighborhood has an "immigrant story" made up of anecdotes and personal dramas in a setting which always included family and church.

In my first book I wrote of growing up with my Irish immigrant grandfather and other great aunts and uncles from the old country.

When I decided to write about my father's side of the family, the Lithuanians, I didn't have the day-to-day wellspring of memories that I had with my mother's side. Through the years, my father and his sisters and brothers often reminisced about the old days in Westfield and the touching memories from that era which, somehow, stayed with me.

Both sets of my grandparents were ordinary people who enriched their surroundings by their individualism. I didn't appreciate until I was an adult that their gift to us was this wonderful country!

Many Americans are not familiar with Lithuania which is one of the three Baltic States located in central Europe. It is roughly the same size as the state of West Virginia. It lies on the edge of the Baltic Sea and shares borders with Belarus, Latvia, Poland and the Russian region of Kaliningrad. Because of its location, Lithuania has been a victim of its powerful neighbors throughout history. It withstood crushing forces from all sides but never lost its determination for survival.

During the period of Russian rule, Lithuania experienced many serious economic, cultural and political hardships. A number of revolts against the Czarist occupation were attempted by various segments of the Lithuanian population.

The actual number of immigrants who came to America from Lithuania is hard to determine because during those times, Lithuanians were considered either Russian, or Polish. This is confirmed by American census records for that period.

My Lithuanian grandparents are listed as being Russian or Lettish which is defined as "of or relating to Latvia". Neither is correct.

The Lithuanians came for various reasons but most found a new home here and established lives for themselves and their families. Their culture and traditions added even more flavor to the "great American melting pot."

TABLE OF CONTENTS

FAMILY DOCUMENTS

GLOSSARY

WESTFIELD LITHUANIANS TODAY

THE BEGINNING

Oh, Ellis Island was swarming
Like a scene from a costume ball,
Decked out in the colors of Europe
On fire with the hope of it all

There my father's own father stood huddled
With the tired and hungry and scared
Turn of the century pilgrims
Bound by the dream that they shared

They were standing in lines just like cattle
Poked and prodded and shoved
Some were one desk away from sweet freedom
Some were torn from someone they love

Through this sprawling tower of Babel
Came a young man confused and alone
Determined and bound for America
And carrying everything that he owned.........

Guy Clark

16

Immigration – the first and second wave

During the nineteenth and early twentieth century, an estimated 300,000 Lithuanians came to America. There were several factors that brought them here. The prominent one was the abolition of serfdom in 1860 which gave Lithuanian peasants a freedom they had never experienced. There was a railroad boom in the late 1850s that made travel easier and, finally, there was a harsh famine in the late 1860s that forced peasants to move in search of money and food.

Most immigrants left on a temporary basis and used their increased income to supplement their farms in Lithuania. They traveled all over Europe and viewed the United States as another place to earn money.

The first wave of immigration from Lithuania, which included my grandfather, began slowly. Small groups of men came here during and after the famine that occurred in the late 1860s. The migration continued in the 1880s and by 1900 had reached a substantial number.

The majority of Lithuanians who left during this time were either young bachelors or married men who left their families to search for work. As 48% were illiterate, they made their living through manual labor. America was just another stop for these men, most of whom never established themselves in any one place but continued to travel from one industrial center to another.

One out of every five Lithuanians who came to America between 1899 and 1914 returned home. Those that stayed gradually established themselves here and formed the links of what historians refer to as chain migration. This refers to the way the Lithuanian-Americans would write home, send tickets and money and invite their friends and relatives to join them in the New World. They sponsored new immigrants and provided them with lodgings and work.

This is confirmed by census records listing boarders in many homes. This habit of inviting friends from the old country helped to establish close-knit Lithuanian communities in America.

In that era, there was a stigma attached to marrying other than a Lithuanian. My Aunt Isabelle, who was born aboard ship on the way to this country, was the only Morris sibling who married another Lithuanian, Adam Dwarska, who was a boarder in their home.

Lithuanian assimilation into American society was gradual. Americans saw them as part of the growing immigration problem at the time. Lithuanians were constantly competing with other immigrants for low-paying manual labor jobs. Life was not easy for them. The language barrier was real and the work was hard.

Lithuanian immigrants helped to establish many unions, including the United Mine Workers of America and the Amalgamated Clothing Workers of America. They became involved in politics and formed their own political parties and societies. They also formed many independent citizens' clubs, fifty of which were organized in New England, including St. Casimir's Society of Westfield, Massachusetts.

The second wave of Lithuanian immigration to the United States came during and after World War II. In 1940, the Soviet Union invaded the Baltic States and Lithuania became the Lithuanian Soviet Socialist Republic .During that period, 30,000 dipukai (war refugees or displaced persons) settled in the midwestern and eastern parts of this country.

In 1941, Germany carried out an invasion of the Soviet Union known as "Operation Barbarossa". Lithuania was once again invaded by Germany. For Lithuanian Jews, this was a disaster. Almost all of Lithuania's 200,000 Jewish citizens were persecuted and murdered as part of the Holocaust.

The Soviet Union regained control in 1944 and stepped up their atrocities and abuses. Farms were seized and farmers forced into slave labor. Many Lithuanian refugees fled westward along with the retreating Germany army. In addition, from 1944-1949, Soviet authorities ordered the deportation of many Lithuanians from their homeland.

As a young kid, I can recall hearing my aunts complaining about the "dp's" (displaced persons)who were taking factory jobs in Westfield. What my aunts and others didn't realize is that most of these immigrants were highly educated professionals in search of a career and their dream was to someday return to their homeland. The Soviet Union imposed persecution, complete dominance and lack of freedom, which explains why so many fled in search of the "American Dream."

COMMUNITY BUILDERS

Westfield Lithuanians

According to city records, the first Lithuanian settler in Westfield, MA was my grandfather, Kazimeras Mereškevičius. He arrived in 1888. His American name was Charles Morris. In 1892, Pranciškus Macijauskas, Simonas Jeglevičius and Jonas Ulinskas rounded out this first small group of immigrants.

Like many Lithuanian immigrants at the turn of the century, they considered their stay in this strange and lonely land as temporary. They hoped to make enough money to begin new lives once again in Lithuania. Their dreams of returning, however, never came to fruition and they did indeed stay and became entrenched in the community.

In 1903, this small group of Lithuanians organized a society choosing St. Casimir to be the patron. This grew into St.Casimir's Church. The constitution for the Lithuanian Mutual Benefit Society indicates that it was founded "so that Lithuanians in a strange country would be able to extend brotherly love toward one another, give aid during misfortunes, visit members who are ill, bury the dead, help the widows and orphans, spread the love of God and neighbors, lead a virtuous life and hold the national spirit among Lithuanians".

Before they had their own parish, most of the Lithuanians attended Mass at the Polish Church in Westfield but once a year, in order to make their Easter duty, a Lithuanian-speaking priest had to be located.

Thanks to the assistance of an Irish priest, Father Fitzgerald, several Lithuanian priests came to Westfield to help the Lithuanians fulfill Lenten obligations. These priests were J. Jakaitis, J. Zebrys, V. Bukaveckas,S.Koloskinskas.P. Meskauskas and J. Ambotas.

Father Jakaitis especially concerned himself with the needs of the Lithuanians in Westfield. He came as often as possible to hear their confessions. He started catechism classes in the Lithuanian language, gave sermons and tried in every way to sustain the religious and secular needs of his compatriots.

Society members built St. Casimir's Hall on William Street in 1915. Council 30 of Knights of Lithuania, which is an American Catholic organization for those of Lithuanian ancestry, was formed at this time. As far back as 1905, St. Casimir's Society had been collecting 25 cents a month from each member for the purpose of establishing a parish. The money they collected was used to purchase land on Parkside and Casimir Streets for a church and rectory.

A delegation was picked to call on Bishop Thomas Beaven for diocesan approval of this undertaking. It took the delegation four trips to the bishop before he gave permission to form a parish and assign any Lithuanian priest that could be found to Westfield. While the church was being built, St. Casimir's Hall was used for weddings, funerals and for Sunday mass. The church had a capacity of 400 and cost $30,000 to build. The first Mass was celebrated on May 30, 1918.

Reverend Constantin Vasys of Worcester, who had been assigned to hear confessions for the Lithuanians, offered his services as pastor of the newly formed parish of St. Casimir. He was followed by Rev. Constantin Strimaitis, Rev. Stasys Vembre,Rev.John Banakas and finally, Rev. Vincent Puidokas who was assigned to St. Casimir in 1934 where he remained pastor until his retirement in 1977.

St. Casimir's was a very active parish and met the spiritual needs of its Lithuanian parishioners for almost 90 years. This small parish neighborhood produced five priests, Rev. John Jutt, Rev. George Naudzius, Rev. Joseph Miller and twin brothers, Rev. Anthony and Rev. Julius Jutt.

My mother recalls some of the traditions at St. Casimir's masses as being very beautiful, especially at Easter, when young girls of the parish would be part of the procession and drop rose petals as they came down the aisle.

Sadly, due to declining membership, this proud Lithuanian church had to close its doors forever on June 8, 2003. Its parishioners merged with St. Peter's Church on State Street, forming a new parish called St. Peter and St. Casimir.

St. Casimir's Church, Westfield, MA

Early days of St. Casimir's circa 1920
(Morris family members are circled)

Blessed Virgin Sodality for young girls of St. Casimir's Parish
with Father Vasys   circa 1924

Kasimeras Mereskevicius
Turn of the century pilgrim

My grandfather wasKazimeras Mereškevičius (Charlie Morris). He came to the United States in 1888 and like many of the Lithuanian immigrants, returned home a few times. On one of his trips home, he got married. He then brought his wife, Josephine Minkle, to this country and settled in Westfield, Massachusetts.

I didn't know my grandfather well as I was 8 or 9 years old when he died. I remember my father bringing me and my two brothers for a ride to Westfield on Sunday mornings to see Grandpa Morris. I can still see him in a small bedroom next to a large kitchen moaning words in Lithuanian that sounded like "woyay" and "woyasu" which. I believe; are roughly translated as "oh god" and "oh Jesus".

My father used to try and converse with him in Lithuanian but my grandfather would reply, "English, Bennie, English." Evidently, my dad didn't retain the language like his sisters did.

A few funny stories were passed down by my mother who lived at the house in Westfield for awhile after she married my father.

At mealtimes whenever they had chicken or any kind of meat on a bone, Charlie, who had very strong teeth, would chew bones down to the marrow. When he was done with a bone, he would give it to their dog to finish off. The story goes that the dog would look at what was left of the bone, look back at my grandfather and walk away.

Another memorable story was during World War II, when his son Lou (Leon) was in the Navy. When Lou would write to him, he would bring the letter to the club (St. Casmir's Society) and read the letter out loud at the bar. "My Louie," he'd say repeatedly through tears. There was a method to his madness as he never had to pay for a drink.

An original saying of Charlie's was his answer to anyone who asked him if he was Polish. He always retorted, "I'm a nickel-plated Polack!" That would be an ethnic slur today but it was his standard answer some 75 years ago. I'm not even sure what it means.

At one point, my uncles Lou and Dud modernized the bathroom on Miller Street. The 1940s popular décor was black wallpaper with pink flamingos and a pink toilet and sink. Lou and Dud showed him the finished room and asked, "What do you think, pop?" His reply was to shake his head and say "lot of money for shithouse!"

I only mention this because I ran into that thinking when I visited Russia in 1991 as a chaperone for my niece and nephew's social studies class. I love Russian history and this trip was amazing! We viewed firsthand the waning days of the USSR in Moscow and Leningrad (now St. Petersburg).

The bathrooms that we encountered on that trip, including those at the Bolshoi Ballet Theater, were very primitive. Our hotel bathrooms had no shower curtains, greasy soap, very stiff tissue paper and ancient plumbing that didn't always work. My grandfather's illustrious words about spending money on bathrooms came to mind often.

Despite his quirks and frugal ways, my grandfather was a true visionary. He was a go-to person in the small Lithuanian community as well as a founder and builder of St. Casmir's Church. According to my father and my Aunt Ann, he spent many weekends working on the new church and purchased one or two of the stained glass windows that remain in the now empty building.

Charlie preserved Lithuanian culture and traditions for future generations the only way he knew how, by devoting his time and his labor to produce something concrete and tangible, e.g., the church, which lasted until 2003. It's written in the Book of Ecclesiastes that *"there's a time to get and a time to lose."* Maybe 90 years in time is the most we can expect from such a legacy .

He also planned and purchased the final resting place for his large family. When my grandmother died in the early 1930s, he bought a plot at St. Mary's Cemetery in Westfield that contains twelve gravesites and has a beautiful rose-colored marble headstone. As of this writing, seven family members are interred there, including my parents and my brother Michael.

Kasimeras Mereškevičius /Charlie Morris

Josephine's Legacy

A triumph of spirit over circumstance

Josephine Minkle Morris came to Westfield with her husband Kazimeras (Charles) before the turn of the century. Her first years as a young wife were difficult. She lived at a time when childbearing was risky for both mother and baby. Of seventeen children born to her, only nine reached adulthood.

Prior to 20th century improvements in sanitation and living standards, children had a high death rate from acute inflammations like measles, scarlet fever, diphtheria, whooping cough, and diarrhea which were real threats to children throughout history and still are in developing countries.

"Every person's a person no matter how small!" I experienced a real sense of loss when I discovered that I had seven uncles and one aunt who never made it past infancy or early childhood.

I am in awe of this strong lady, my grandmother, who was able to confront the recurring presence of sorrow in her life and still prevail. It became a sadly familiar task for her to prepare a baby for burial after which there was no time to grieve. She had to pick up the pieces and keep things going in the family.

There were numerous daily chores including tending to large gardens, feeding the animals, meal preparation, cleaning and generally taking care of her husband and nine surviving children Isabelle, Michael, Mary(May), Nelly(El),Annie(Ann), Benjamin, Leon(Lou),George(Dud)andHelena (Helen).

Being part of a large family in those days meant leaving school at a young age and going to work to help out at home. If there was a goal that this family aspired to it was getting a good job and having your own home. Eventually, every member of the Morris family reached that goal.

Note: to my lost aunt and uncles: Petrenella, Peter, James, Joseph, Walter, Charles, John and Alexander Morris; I wish members of my generation had known some of you. You would have really liked your brothers. My father, Ben, Mike, Lou and Dud, to a man, had tough guy exteriors, but were real marshmallows when it came to family. Your sister Annie would have been a joy to know!

Maybe some of you would have been musical like the rest of the family and would have loved dancing and singing. Maybe one of you would have gone into politics and made a difference in the everyday lives of your family and others. I'm so sorry that you never had the chance to find your place in the world.

Josephine Minkle Morris

Fifty years on Miller Street
a time of pigs, chickens, mellow apples and rock gardens

Charles & Josephine Minkle Morris lived at 13 Miller Street in Westfield beginning in the early 1900's. Miller Street then, like the rest of the neighborhood, was a melting pot of immigrants—with Slavic, Lithuanian, Polish and Russian roots and many others.

Some of the names on the census records from 1910 to 1930 were Morris (Mereškevičius), Balakounis, Amberlok Unitas, Snyder, Jegawicz,Tysz, Kardel, Dwarska, Rogescius, Dardinski, Masaitis, Danyla,Jonaitis,Minkus,Olinski,Jaculkus, etc. No matter what part of Europe they came from, they were all sustained and nourished by faith, family and the promises of America.

Imagine being a census taker in those days; trying to write down information given to you by residents who spoke limited English with various accents. My guess is that children's names were written as they sounded. My aunt Isabelle was written as Zabelia, which may have been what she was called by her immigrant parents.

Life on Miller Street was pretty much like most communities in the early1900s. Miller Street is off of Meadow Street where there were numerous ethnic storefronts that sold homemade bread and other groceries though much of the food for each family was provided by large gardens and animals___pigs, cows, goats and chickens.

My Aunt Ann told of the many times that her mother, Josie, would have a bunch of ladies gather in their yard to see the latest fabrics from the local peddler of yard goods who traveled around by horse and wagon. She remembers her favorite material being crepe de chine.

In addition to gardens, the Morris family had a large grape arbor and apple trees, which my father referred to as "mellow" apples. My research on mellow apples indicates that they are a smaller low-acid fruit that ripens later around Thanksgiving. My brother and I remember those mellow apples as being yellow and softer than golden delicious apples.

The rock garden at 13 Miller Street with its abundant flowers was the centerpiece of the Morris yard. It had several large rocks which can best be described as rocks of ages with unusual shapes. One resembled an anvil, one was flat with a round raised part in the middle that looked like a mushroom and one was waterworn into several levels. They originally came from the banks of the Westfield River.

When the house was sold in the 1960s, my father hauled some of the rocks to our home in Springfield. After my parents passed on, my brother moved two of the rocks to his yard in New Hampshire and my sister took one for her yard in East Longmeadow.

Another lasting memento is one of the pews from St. Casimir's Church which ended up in the eastern Massachusetts home of Mary Morris Parody's son, Michael, whose wife grew up in the parish.

In 1913, my grandfather was accused of stealing a pig. There was a long detailed story in the local newspaper at the time. It seems my grandmother was walking home to Miller Street after visiting a friend

on Chapel Street when she heard
something running after her and snorting.
She was terrified. She ran home and told
my grandfather that a "sure devil" was
chasing her.

My grandfather went out and saw a
large pig in his tomato patch. He scooped
up the pig and showed my grandmother the
"devil" that was chasing her. Just at that
moment, the owners of the pig, who lived
on Otis Street, looked out their window and
saw Charlie holding their pig.

The husband and wife rushed over
to Miller Street and accused him of stealing
the animal. Evidently, my grandfather lost
his temper and told them he would "lick"
them for their accusations. The police were
called to settle the dispute. The result was
my grandfather being fined ten dollars for
pig larceny and another ten dollars for
assault and battery. That had to be a lot of
money in those days!

An article in the 1937 paper involved
my uncle, Mike Morris. who was a truck
driver for many years. He was driving a
truckload of woolens to New York City
when some hijackers jumped into the cab of

his truck. They made him drive to a garage where they tied him up and put duct tape over his mouth and left him with the truck.

My uncle managed to get out of the truck and hop over to the locked door of the garage and bang on it until someone heard him and called the police. The police were waiting for the hijackers when they returned.

I had always heard that Mike Morris was a very tough guy in his prime. He was big and had a snarly voice and backed down to no one, but was a real sweetheart to friends and family. I remember that he was a caring uncle to my siblings and me. He was especially close to my father during some hard times.

Miller Street is very close to the Westfield River. My father often talked about swimming in the Westfield River. Learning to swim consisted of being thrown in the river by older siblings and told to "sink or swim."

Before dikes, dams and pumping stations were built, there was always a danger of flooding whenever the river rose over its banks. The great hurricane of 1938 brought very heavy downpour which resulted in massive flooding. The streets were impassable in anything but a boat. My mother was evacuated from 13 Miller Street in a rowboat when she was seven months pregnant with my brother Dick.

Ironically, this may have been a premonition of the future. Dick went on to a career in the US Coast Guard and spent many years on the water from the Atlantic Ocean to the Arctic Ocean and beyond.

Miller Street today has changed. Like all city neighborhoods, there are houses where there once were lots and open spaces and the neighborhood is made up of different immigrant groups.

Ben Morris and "Teddy" Miller St. rock garden 1935

Dick Morris   Miller St. rock garden 1939

Rocks moved from Miller Street to Springfield and finally to the New Hampshire home of Dick Morris 2016

anvil rock

Mushroom rock

Keeping Traditions-Kūĉios"

Traditional Christmas Eve celebration

My mother often shared memories of Christmas Eve at my father's house when they were dating. Kūĉios is the Lithuanian tradition of celebrating Christmas Eve and is the last day of fasting for Advent.

My mother recalled a large roasted pig with an apple in its mouth as the centerpiece of the table, though she never remembers it being served. Natalie Masaitis and Jim and Marcia Rogers, all of whom grew up with this tradition, assured me that Christmas eve was a meatless celebration. Ham was served the next day for Christmas dinner.

Natalie Masaitis remembers washing her father's hammer so it could be used to smash poppy seeds into milk.which they would have with small pieces of baked dough about ½ inch thick made by her mother. Her family would always have traditional beet soup, herring, haddock and boiled potatoes. Dessert was a fruit compote.

Marcia Rogers told of similar traditions in her family. They had herring,smelts, beet soup, baked haddock, boiled potatoes, pierogies filled with farmer's cheese, potatoes or cabbage, sauerkraut salad, rye bread and a sweet Christmas bread with raisins. Dessert was cranberry pudding and fruit compote.

They all remember starting the meal by saying grace and the head of the family breaking the communion wafer (plotkele) blessed by the parish priest. The wafer was then passed to each person at the table to break off a piece, then the children would pass it to cousins and other relatives until everyone had a piece of the blessed wafer.

According to Marcia Rogers, Father Puidokas used to invite Lithuanian priests from around the state to celebrate Kūĉios at the St. Casimir's rectory. The cook at the rectory, Onate, made all the traditional LIthuanian dishes which were very much enjoyed by the visiting priests.

Father Puidokas

Shepherd, patriot, friend

No history of the St. Casimir family would be complete without acknowledging the influence and contributions of Father Vincent Puidokas.

Father Puidokas was the pastor for St. Casimir's Church beginning in 1934 until 1977. He was the last pastor of Lithuanian ancestry. The common language was one of the strengths that preserved the flavor of the church community.

He was a true man of God and could be a stern leader of his flock but he could always be counted on for help whether it was for spiritual guidance or financial assistance.

In 1939, he became the first priest in Western Mass to receive a pilot's license. In his words, he learned to fly in order to "move with the times."

He revitalized and took an active role in the Knights of Lithuania Council 30 and personally worked with members to write letters to Congress demanding recognition of the Republic of Lithuania.

Father was on top of everything that went on in the parish. He knew every family as he visited their homes once a year to update parish membership cards. He handpicked Sunday school instructors and other volunteers that were vital to the day-to-day operation of the church. On holidays, he passed the basket himself, thus encouraging everyone to dig deeper.

Though he lived in the rectory, Father owned a rustic cottage and a boat on Congamond Lake in Southwick. He was very generous in allowing parishioners to use the cottage for a weekend. He also let the girl scouts have campouts there. He loved the young people of the parish and referred to them as my" kiddos".

Father was a staunch patron of St. Anthony's Monastery in Kennebunkport, Maine. St. Anthony's was purchased by the Lithuanian branch of the Franciscan monks in 1947 and by 1952, a monastery and guest house was established. To this day, there is a dining hall where wonderful Lithuanian dishes are served.

Father Puidokas personally funded the construction of the Stations of the Cross which are embedded in the walls of the Chapel on the grounds of the monastery. Since its inception, Council 30 members have enjoyed retreats in Maine at this scenic place.

On a personal note, I had occasion to visit St. Anthony's. One summer, my family and I discovered it by accident as we were looking for a motel in Kennebunkport, Maine. I enjoyed the beautiful grounds and the Lithuanian food that is served and was amazed at the number of guests including children that spoke Lithuanian to each other.

Their gift shop had jewelry made from amber which is found along the coast of Lithuania. My daughter was fascinated with the pieces that had ants trapped inside of them.

Father Puidokas' retirement marked the end of an era. After his departure, the church was staffed with various priests, the last one being Father Daniel Foley. Father Puidokas resided in a nursing home for many years until his death in the 1980s. His funeral mass was held at St. Casimir's, the church he loved and served for 43 years of his life.

THE REVEREND VINCENT PUIDOKAS — Pastor of St. Casimir's Parish

Father Vincent Puidokas

LITHUANIAN INFLUENCE

Lithuanian Contributions to America

As mentioned previously, Lithuanian contributions to this country include forming the United MIne Workers union and the United Garment Workers union. Throughout the century, Lithuanians slowly began to climb up the economic ladder. Lithuanians also became active in the military and have served in every battle. Because of the direct effect both world wars had on Lithuanian freedom, the United States military saw a large turnout of Lithuanian soldiers.

The first director of the FBI, Bruce Bialaski, was an American of Lithuanian descent. Actors Laurence Harvey, Charles Bronson and Sean Penn, actress Ruta Lee and legendary singer Bob Dylan, all with Lithuanian roots, have made significant contributions to American films and music.

Johnny Unitas was one of the greatest quarterbacks of the National Football League and Dick Butkus was probably the best middle linebacker ever to play the game. They are both Americans of

Lithuanian descent and both are in the Football Hall of Fame.

Sarunas Maciuliois started his basketball career with Staytba Vilnius in 1981. He moved to the United States in 1989 to play professionally for California's Golden State Warriors, Denver Nuggets, Seattle and Sacramento. He is in the Basketball Hall of Fame. After the earthquake in San Francisco in 1989, Maciuliois helped to pull out passengers trapped in a train.

LITHUANIA THEN AND NOW

The Long Road to Independence

Lithuania and its people have had many struggles over the last few hundred years. But, despite occupation and invasion, Lithuania has held on to the idea of itself as an independent union.

From 1944 to 1952, well-organized military units of the Lithuanian resistance movement waged a guerilla war against the Soviet military. Fifty thousand lives were lost on each side. This went on until the 1970s, when a national and religious dissent, unrivaled in all of the Soviet Union, emerged. After 40 years of Soviet rule, a prolific underground press revealed deep-seated opposition to the Soviet system.

The rise of Mikhail Gorbachev to the Soviet leadership and his plans to restructure society and loosen political controls led to the emergence of national democratic movements.

In 1989, the Lithuanians joined the Latvians and Estonians to form a two million person human chain of protest. Two million people linked hands stretching from

Tallinn on the Gulf of Finland to Vilnius. They declared that Soviet annexation was against the will of the citizens of the Baltic States and that the illegal German-Soviet agreements of 1939-1941 were an international crime. Even the Congress of the Soviet Union acknowledged the illegality of the Nazi-Soviet pact.

The Lithuanian parliament was given a mandate to reestablish the independence of their nation by an overwhelming majority of the electorate. They became independent on September 6, 1991 and became members of the UN. They also joined the European Union EU and NATO.

In 1990, a Professor of Music, Vytautas Landsbergis, was elected Chairman of the Supreme Council of Lithuania. He was a non-communist and founder of *Sajūdis* (a political organization which led the struggle for Lithuanian independence in the late 1980s and early 1990s. He was a true hero and played a crucial role in the confrontation between the Lithuanian Independence Movement and Soviet armed forces in January 1991.

Landsbergis was a conservative politician and an activist who served as Speaker of the *Seimas*(Lithuanian Parliament) from 1996 until 2000. In 2004, he was elected by Lithuanian voters to the European Parliament in Brussels where he served two terms. Currently, his grandson, Gabrielius Landsbergis represents Lithuania in the European Parliament.

In the 1992 Olympics held in Barcelona,Spain, the Lithuanian basketball team became the "other dream team" of those games. Their newly independent nation was financially strapped and not able to pay the expenses for the team's participation. The late Jerry Garcia and his famous band, *The Grateful Dead*, heard of the team's plight and paid for uniforms and other expenses.

The Lithuanian basketball team won the bronze medal that year and Grateful Dead band members were on hand to celebrate their victory.

The now famous shirts from those Olympics were tie-dyed in the Lithuanian colors with the Grateful Dead skeleton dunking a basket. They are very symbolic of a nation rising from the dead. Sales of these tie-dyed shirts not only helped the team but also children's charities in Lithuania. The shirts served as goodwill ambassadors.

The new government of Lithuania instituted many changes in 1991 which led to a more western-style society, but jobs were hard to find at first and many people were poor. But, by the early part of the twenty-first century, the economy was booming!

This lasted until 2008 when the global economy crashed. Lithuania was hit hard and unemployment reached 14%. By 2009, it slowly recovered. Lithuanians have held on to their culture and traditions throughout their difficult history and are looking ahead to the future.

Unfortunately, as of this writing, there are rumblings that Vladimir Putin wants to control the Baltic States economically and politically through a wide network of former KGB agents and other clandestine activities.

Professor Landsbergis continues to be a fierce critic of Russia's intentions to impose any kind of influence on the Baltics and publicly questions their actions in both local and international media, as well as the European Parliament.

He is still an active politician who once petitioned Russia to compensate Lithuania and other post-Soviet republics for damage done to them during occupation.

Natalie Masaitis reports that this "saber rattling" has her relatives and friends in Lithuania very upset and afraid for the future.

EARLY RESEARCH

The Sociology of a Family

Joan Morris Reilly

This paper was successfully submitted for credit in the Elms College LEAF Program (Life Experience Application Forum) in 1994

Where does a family begin? What forces shape the personalities that make up a family? What conditions govern the thinking, beliefs, occupations and resulting lifestyle of a family? What traits show up in other generations?

Thanks to genealogy classes, public records, family photographs and asking a lot of questions, I can trace my family to the late 1800s on my paternal side. My grandfather Charles Morris, (renamed at Ellis Island-original name, Kazimeras Meriskevicius) emigrated from Lithuania, then a territory of Russia. He came by ship via Hamburg, Germany, according to his application for citizenship.

One has to wonder how he got from Vilnius on the Baltic Sea to Germany-horse and buggy,train, on foot? Unfortunately, he came through Ellis Island before they kept records which was started in 1898.

My maternal grandfather, James J. Cabey, came to this country from Ireland by steerage through the port of Boston in 1901. He was a young man of 17 coming to a place where "Irish need not apply".

So, one grandfather landed in New York and could speak several languages Lithuanian, Russian, Polish and Yiddish but not English, which set him apart from the natives. The other came to Boston where Catholicism (papists) and Irish were scorned by the Brahmin/wasp element.

One settled in Westfield, Massachusetts, the first Lithuanian on record to do so. He later made several trips back to Lithuania. On one of these trips, he brought back a wife Josephine Minkle, "Jusea" who delivered a child enroute to this new land. Charles eventually applied for and became a citizen. My father recalls his father and several other Lithuanians attending citizenship classes at night.

There is no record of Josephine becoming a citizen. I believe when a man became a citizen in those days, citizenship was automatically granted to his wife. Charles went to work for a thriving industry in Westfield, Pope Manufacturing, later to become Columbia Bicycle.

Josephine's life could best be described in today's terms as physically challenging. It consisted of backbreaking work from dawn to dusk. As they grew all of their own food there were large gardens and fruit trees to tend followed by harvesting and canning. There were chickens and pigs to raise and eventually slaughter for food.

There were yearly additions to their growing family: nine children survived 17 pregnancies. One of the few breaks in her routine was preparing a child's body, usually an infant, for burial eight different times! Josephine died in her early 50s. She must have been worn out physically from numerous pregnancies and hard labor, not to mention the unbelievable mental anguish of losing so many babies to the diseases of the times. Charles, on the other hand, lived to be 88 years old and died with a full head of hair and all of his teeth!

My Irish grandfather settled in Springfield, Mass where a sister resided and worked at his trade. He was a blacksmith according to the city directory of 1910. He eventually married another Irish immigrant who lived in Lowell, Mass, Agnes Frawley. They had four children. Tragically, Agnes contracted Bright's disease, a kidney disorder, and died at age 42, six weeks after the birth of their fourth child.

James then worked full time at the Indian Motorcycle plant and attempted to raise 4 children with the assistance of hired housekeepers. Not all of them were good. My aunt Marie left school at age 11 and assumed the responsibilities of the household and caring for the younger children.

Though James was a handsome, considerate young man, remarriage was not an option in his mind. It certainly would have been a solution under the circumstances. He lived to be 72 years old.

Prevalent on the Morris side was the uneven distribution of offspring. All nine married and had a total of 21 children, seven of which belonged to my father. Two sisters and a brother did not have children and the sisters that did have children had problems, i.e., 3 stillborns, including a set of twins. The oldest sister had a child who had epileptic seizures and due to the times, was kept out of sight, not educated and eventually institutionalized.

There was only one broken marriage in this generation, an older brother who was an alcoholic and left his family for many years. Life-threatening illness occurred twice. A younger sister had tuberculosis and was hospitalized for a long period. Another sister had breast cancer 20 years ago but is alive and well in her 80s today.

The four Cabeys all married and three had children for an impressive total of 18! None were plagued with life-threatening illness though the youngest son, in middle age, developed a serious skin disorder that led to the breakdown of his immune system. He eventually lost a leg to circulatory problems. He survived another year or two and died at age 68.

Of all the family members mentioned above, nine Morris family members and four Cabeys, the only one that had a high school education was my mother.

The rest completed their formal education at a young age, around sixth or seventh grade. They were expected to work and help out financially. Their jobs were blue collar, mostly factory workers, truck drivers, a cook, a mechanic, security guard, etc. Three of this group of 13 served in the military and one participated in a CCC camp. They were all hard workers and all were basically in the same socio- economic class. Owning their own home was the yardstick by which they measured success and every one of them qualified.

Collectively, their taste in music ran to the music of the day, late 1930s and 40s vintage. Several of them could play instruments (self-taught) and all loved to sing and were good dancers, also self taught.

Religion (Catholicism) was important in their lives, not in a controlling way but present in the ceremonial sense, at the weddings, baptisms and funerals that marked the passages of time in a family.

My grandfather Morris was one of the founders and builders of the Lithuanian Church, St. Casmir's, in Westfield. In summary, this generation of my family can all be described as strong, industrious, law abiding good people who worked hard and played equally hard. All enjoyed drinking, especially at family gatherings. Despite this love of spirits, only one or two problem drinkers emerged.

Upward mobility, consisting chiefly of a high school education, was expected and achieved with a few exceptions by the next generation of 32 persons; 21 Morris offspring and 11 Cabeys. A few of these 32 have a college education.

The changing times brought some of life's disappointments and pain to this new generation. Alcoholism, homosexuality, heart disease and at least seven divorces have all made an appearance in this group of 32. Two have died and one is presumed to be dead as he has been missing for over 20 years.

On the plus side, the occupations went up a notch corporate accountant, dental hygienist, nurse, nuclear inspector, graphic artist, teacher, administrative assistant, publishing executive, TV reporter/public relations representative and a few entrepreneurs.

With few exceptions, this generation is still very much a part of the working class as opposed to being members of a profession.

A few have travelled extensively and broadened their horizons and have expanded their outlooks. Two fought in and survived an unpopular war. Five others served peace-time hitches in the military, one making it a 26-year career. Though most are homeowners, this was not the ultimate achievement for this group that it was for their elders.

Thanks to modern media, they are, as a group, better informed and better educated than their parents. In some but not in all cases, tastes have expanded to include art and other types of music and literature. There are many good singing voices and some talented instrumentalists in this generation.

This generation of 32 men and women had a total of 58 offspring and some of these offspring have started yet another generation. The future of this group of 58 remains to be seen.

The oldest of these are young men and women in their early to mid 30s and the youngest is one year old. A college degree is already the norm for this group of young people. At least 14 have graduated from college and several are enrolled in college at this writing. It will be interesting to compare the occupations and activities of this new group

.

I hope to keep track of the happenings in their lives and record it for posterity. I'm the self-appointed guardian of the thread that connects each generation of this family. It's a labor of love as well as an interesting way to spend leisure time.

Family Documents

Charlie Morris application for citizenship

Form 2203
U. S. DEPARTMENT OF LABOR
NATURALIZATION SERVICE

TRIPLICATE
(To be given to the person the Declaration)

No. 14334

UNITED STATES OF AMERICA

DECLARATION OF INTENTION

☞ Invalid for all purposes seven years after the date hereof

Commonwealth of Massachusetts ⎫
⎬ ss.:
Hampden County ⎭

In the ___Superior___

of ___Hampden County___

I, ___Kasimireas Merszkevicz alias Charles Morris___, aged ___53___
occupation ___Laborer___, do declare on oath that my pe...
description is: Color ___white___, complexion ___Medium___, height ___5___ feet ___6___ in...
weight ___175___ pounds, color of hair ___Brown___, color of eyes ___Blue___
other visible distinctive marks ___None___
I was born in ___Olava, Russia___
on the ___4___ day of ___March___, anno Domini 1 ___866___; I now re...
at ___13 Miller St., Westfield, Mass.___
I emigrated to the United States of America from ___Bremen, Germany___
on the vessel ___unknown___
foreign residence was ___Svoliskos, Russia___; I am ___married; the...
of my wife is ___Josephine___; she was born at ___Olava, Russia___
and now resides at ___said 13 Miller St.___
It is my bona fide intention to renounce forever all allegiance and fidelity to any fo...
prince, potentate, state, or sovereignty, and particularly to ___The Present Governm...
of Russia___, of whom I am now a sub...
I arrived at the port of ___New York___
State of ___New York___, on or about the ___15___
of ___April___, anno Domini 1 ___893___; I am not an anarchist; I am n...
polygamist nor a believer in the practice of polygamy; and it is my intention in good...
to become a citizen of the United States of America and to permanently reside th...
SO HELP ME GOD.

charly morri...

(Original signature of declarant)

Subscribed and sworn to before me in the office of the Cl...
said Court this ___18___ day of ___April___, anno Domini...

[SEAL]

Robert O. Morri...

Clerk of the ___Superior___

89

TITION OF
Kazimirsas
svevicz
TES OF AMERICA.

Filed ___September 27___, 19 21

OATH OF ALLEGIANCE

I absolutely and entirely renounce and abjure all allegiance and fidelity to any foreign prince, po...
y to __Russia or any independent state within the bounds of the former__
Russian Empire
bject; that I will support and defend the Constitution and laws of the United States of America aga...
that I will bear true faith and allegiance to the same.

s *mereszkiavic*   *Charles Morris*

e me, in open Court, this __27__ day of __March__, A. D. 19 22

Charles M Calhoun asst. Ci

e following to the oath of allegiance before it is executed: "I further renounce the title of (give title), an order of nobility, which I have here...

ORDER OF COURT ADMITTING PETITIONER

tition of ____Charles Morris____, and affidavits in support there...
urt, it is ordered that the said petitioner, who has taken the oath required by law, be, and hereby is, ad...
ates of America, this __27__ day of __March__, A. D. 19 22
nsideration of the petition of the said _____, that his na...
_____ under authority of the provisions of section 6 of the act ap...
6), as amended by the act approved March 4, 1913, entitled "An act to create a Department of Labor."

C J Callahan, Justic

Receipt for 12 gravesites at St. Mary's Cemetery

St. Mary's Cemetery.

Westfield, Mass., *March 4,* 1930

$ 35. 00/100

This certifies that *Charles Monio*

having paid *thirty-five* dollars, the receipt
whereof is hereby acknowledged, and having moreover
agreed to the conditions herein mentioned, is hereby
entitled to the possession of Plot No. *280*
in Range ———— Section *5* of St. Mary's
Cemetery of Westfield, Mass.

12 graves

Conditions

1. All persons to be interred in the aforesaid Cemetery must be baptized, and be understood as belonging to the Roman Catholic Faith, and in no wise under the ban of excommunication from whatsoever cause.

2. The aforesaid plot must be always subject to the control which the Roman Catholic Church has over said Cemetery, and to all the rules and regulations which have been made, or shall be made in relation to said Cemetery and the mode of burial therein.

3. Every headstone, monument, or other memorial of the dead must be of Roman Catholic design and meet the Pastor's approval.

4. The pastor reserves to himself the right of preventing or removing any erection or enclosure which he may deem injurious to the immediate locality, or prejudicial to the general appearance of the Cemetery; and of removing or pruning any trees or shrubbery which may mar the beauty of the grounds, or which will interfere with other plots or graves.

5. Persons who have died bereft of reason in consequence of drunkenness, fallen in duel, wilfully departed life without having received the Sacraments, or having been in any way opposed to the Roman Catholic Church, shall be debarred from all rights and privileges otherwise conveyed by this instrument.

6. This Deed must be presented to the Superintendent when a grave is to be opened in the within named lot.

Rev. J. H. Freel
Acting Rector

Thomas Cusack
Superintendent

91

Local newspaper 1913

Public Sunday, September 7, 1913   Pappers Springfield Daily News (Springfield, MA)   Page: 15
This entire product and/or portions thereof are copyrighted by Readbest and/or the American Antiquarian Society. 2013.
Source: Genealogybank.com

~~~ ·DAILY NEWS, MONDA~

DEVIL APPEARS
IN FORM OF PIG

Charles Morris Is Fined $10 for Stealing "Satan" and $10 for Assault

ON OWNERS OF PORKER

Westfield, Sept. 8.—The devil appeared here last evening with four legs, a grunt and a squeal and chased Mrs. Charles Morris down Chapel, Mechanic and White streets to her home on Miller street, and the "bad man" was finally captured in the Morris tomato patch, according to the story told by Morris as he reached the police station last evening after he had been arrested on the charge of the larceny of

5/1/2014 12

92

a pig belonging to Dennis Moran of Otis street.

Morris claimed that his wife had been visiting on Chapel street, and that as she came on that street to return to her home she heard a grunt behind her and also heard several squeals, which, she claimed, were from a "sure devil." She ran to her home as fast as she could and told her husband about the animal or object that had been chasing her.

Morris went out of the house and heard the devil in his tomato patch. After many squeals and grunts had been heard he returned to his house with a pig in his arms, which, he said, was the devil that had been chasing his wife.

The other side of the devil story came from Dennis Moran; who declared in District Court this morning that his pet pig had been stolen from its pen on Otis street by Morris. Moran said that he was looking out of his window and saw Morris marching to Morris's home with the latter's pig in his arms. Moran and his wife followed Morris to his home and demanded the pig, but Morris showed fight and attempted to "lick" the Moran family.

The police were called in to help matters along, and Officers Michael Condon and Patrick Coffey had to escort Morris to the police station, where he narrated his story about the devil chasing his wife, thus accounting for his strange actions in refusing to give up the pig to Mr. Moran.

As an after-incident to the devil, or pig, story Morris was fined $10 for the larceny of the pig and $10 for assault and battery upon Mr. and Mrs. Moran.

Date: Friday, May 28, 1937   **Paper:** Springfield Republic.
This entire product and/or portions thereof are copyrighted by NewsBank

West

TRUCK DRIVER OUTWITS BANDITS, SAVES LOAD

Michael Morris Foils Attempt to Hijack $10,000 Cargo of Woolen Goods

New York, May 27—Michael Morris of Westfield, put one over on three bandits who hijacked his $10,000 truckload of woolens today.

The hijackers jumped aboard his truck as he was driving through the busy woolen goods district and forced him to come to a halt. Then they blindfolded and gagged Morris and took him along with the trailer-truck to a garage where they dumped the woolens.

They drove off again and abandoned Morris and his truck. But Morris managed to slip the blindfold off one eye and he noted the address of the garage. Still gagged, he summoned police by banging on the door. They all returned to the garage and recovered the woolens.

GLOSSARY OF LITHUANIAN WORDS

Lithuanian words and phrases
Translated by Natalie Masaitis

English	Lithuanian
hello	labas
good bye	sudiev
thank you	aciu
you're welcome	prasom
mother	molina
father	levas
sister	sesuo
brother	brolis
love	meili

how are you	kaip tau seikasi
how's it going	kaip tau einas
(reply) fine, thanks gerai	aciu
please	prasau
good morning rytas	labas
my name is vardas	mano
pleased to meet you sutikti	malonu
cheers, good health	sveikata
good luck	laimi

family	seima
yes	taip jo
No	Ne
grandpa	Senelis
grandma	senele
	or senule
friend	drauge(
	(fem)
	draugus
	masc.

WESTFIELD LITHUANIANS
TODAY

Lithuanian descendants keep the culture alive

Council 30 Knights of Lithuania was formed in 1915. Due to World War I and lack of leadership, it became inactive in 1917. When Reverend Vincent Puidokas was assigned to St. Casimir's church, he reactivated Council 30 and membership grew steadily with a slump during World War II, peaking in the 1970s with fifty plus members.

The motto of Knights of Lithuania is "For God and Country." Their reason for being is to keep alive an appreciation of the Lithuanian language, customs and culture while stressing the importance of Roman Catholic beliefs.

Throughout the many years of forced Russian domination C30 supported efforts urging members to write letters to their Congressmen demanding recognition of the existence of "The Republic of Lithuania" and its freedom from the USSR.

They have supported Camp Neringa in Vermont, St. Casimir's   Pontifical

Lithuanian College in Rome and the Children's Lithuanian Relief Aid. Members served as teachers for CCD and First Communion classes. Flowers are provided for all religious occasions.

The officers and members of Council 30 are keeping old traditions alive and still make Lithuanian kielbasa (desru) with their secret recipe at Easter. Current officers are President Marcia Rogers, Vice President, Janet Thyburg, Secretary, Barbara Sokolowski, Treasurer James Rogers, Culture, William Miller and Scribe, Carol Miller.

Council 30 is now much smaller but remains very committed with two fourth-degree members and four third-degree members.

They have been represented at many National Conventions. They take part in the annual Maironis Park festival in Shrewsbury,MA and attend Friendship Day, which is sponsored by the Sisters of Immaculate Conception Order in Putnam, Connecticut. At both gatherings, Lithuanian food and drink and dancers are featured.

St. Peter St. Casimir Church, a 2003 merger of Slovak and Lithuanian parishes on State Street, Westfield

ST. CASIMIR'S SOCIETY

FEBRUARY 9, 1985

SONS OF ERIN

ST. CASIMIR'S MEMBERS HAVE FOR MANY YEARS PAUSED TO
PALM THIS CORNER OF THE BAR IN FRIENDSHIP. OFFICERS OF THE
SONS OF ERIN CARESS THIS SYMBOL OF BROTHERHOOD — THAT
WE MAY SERVE OUR MEMBERS IN THE SAME PROUD TRADITION
AS THE ST. CASIMER'S SOCIETY HAS SERVED THEIRS.
MAY WE SHARE AN ETERNITY OF FRIENDSHIP.

St. Casmir's Hall was built in 1915 by the
Lithuanians. It was used for social gatherings and
for Sunday mass before the church was built. This
plaque of recognition hangs in the now Sons of
Erin Hall.   Photo courtesy of Joe Christofori

Let us sing of days gone by

Blood and tears to sanctify
Freedom was a lullaby
When they made the crossing......

As they turned from hunger's door
Troubles there to bear no more
Promise waiting on the shore
For those who made the crossing

Some would rise and some would fall
Battle cry they heard the call
Liberty was after all
Why they made the crossing.........

So raise a glass and speak the names
All of those who braved the flames
Heaven, hell it's all the same
For those who made the crossing

Willie Nile